the art of STENCILLING

by Helen Barnett

ISBN 1 871517 25 7

Osmiroid Creative Leisure Series

About the Author

Helen Barnett is the Home Editor of Ideal Home magazine, and is involved with writing all kinds of features on the more practical aspects of decorating and running a home.

After studying Home Economics at Sheffield Polytechnic, Helen joined IPC magazines in 1979 and worked first in the home department of Women and Home before moving to Homes and Gardens as home economist. She went to Ideal Home as Deputy home editor in May 1983 and was promoted to Home Editor in November 1987.

Helen teamed up with journalist and designer Susy Smith in 1986 to write her first book on stencilling.

The Osmiroid Stencilling Kit provides everything you need to start creating exciting stencils. As your interest and skill in the art of stencilling grows, you may wish to purchase other materials to develop some of the further ideas outlined in this book as well as your own particular interests.

CONTENTS

WHAT IS STENCILLING?

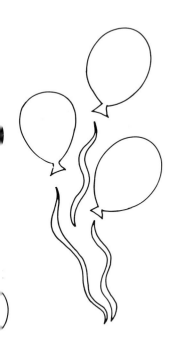

The art of stencilling, now enjoying renewed popularity, is basically a very simple means of reproducing imaginative and unusual patterns by hand. You can use it to decorate all kinds of surfaces; walls, floors, furniture and fabrics, but you won't need to spend a lot of money initially on materials and equipment, and you'll be able to pick up the basic techniques very quickly.

A stencil is made from impervious material. The design that you wish to reproduce is cut out of the material, and colour (usually paint) is then applied through these cut out shapes. The areas of material between the cut out sections of the stencil are called bridges. These not only strengthen the stencil itself but turn what would otherwise be a silhouette into a recognisable motif.

In this book we take you through the basic techniques involved in mastering the art of stencilling. We show you the essential tools you'll need, explain exactly how to use a stencil and take you through a series of projects designed to help you gain confidence in your newly acquired skills, and give you some ideas for the application of stencils. We even tell you how to make your own stencils and create unusual special effects.

The Art of Stencilling is the perfect companion to the Osmiroid Stencilling Kit, which not only contains a set of essential equipment, but four ready cut stencils depicting the designs in the project section. Use these to practice your skills, you'll be amazed at how easy it is to create professional looking results.

The History of Stencilling

Very little is known about the true origins of stencilling. Many believe that the Chinese were the first to use the process as long ago as 3000 B.C., others that the Egyptians originated the art 500 years later to decorate the coffins of their dead. It is difficult to pinpoint any precise beginnings because the earliest stencils were probably made from perishable materials such as leaves and animal skins. But the principles of the art are so simple it is likely that most of the ancient cultures would have developed their own form of stencilling as a method of making pattern.

The Chinese invented paper around 105 A.D., and after this more accurate dating could be given to the use of stencils. With the opening up of the Eastern trade routes the popularity of stencilling quickly spread, first to countries like Japan and India and then to Europe where it was most widely used as a decoration on playing cards in Italy and France. The word stencil is in fact believed to come from the old French word 'estenceler' (to sparkle), and the latin 'scintilla' (a spark).

Stencilling was first used in England around the 13th or 14th century to decorate the walls of medieval churches. Later, in Tudor and Jacobean times it was used to create simple geometric patterns on the walls of large manor houses, and it remained a popular method of decoration for many centuries.

In the early 17th century French craftsmen began to develop the first wallpapers using the basic techniques of stencilling. These 'flock' papers, made to copy expensive tapestries and wall brocades, were created using a stencil template through which a coloured glue was applied and pieces of shredded wool were sprinkled to give a raised textured pattern. The wallpapers could only be made on relatively small pieces of paper however and were very expensive to buy. Not until the mid 19th century when paper tax was removed and wallpaper could be made on continuous rolls, did it become a cheaper form of decoration. Throughout the 17th, 18th and early 19th centuries however direct stencilling on to walls remained a popular and economic form of decoration for the less wealthy.

At the time when stencilling was at its greatest prominence in Europe, the early settlers of North America adopted it as a form of more refined decoration for their houses. Initially designs were produced by imaginative housewives, but as more complicated patterns became popular, bands of 'professional' decorators grew up, travelling the country transforming plain interiors with a wealth of pattern and colour. These early American stencils used on walls, floors, furniture and fabrics, had an individual, naive charm, taking their inspiration from the flowers, fruit and birds of the countryside.

Gradually as industrialization progressed and demand for stencilled products increased, commercially produced fabrics, carpet and wallpapers replaced the work of individual craftsmen.

Stencilling remained popular until as late as the second World War when the trend for plain interiors meant it largely died out. But with the recent revival in traditional crafts and paint techniques it is again enjoying a renewed interest, and can be seen in many modern homes.

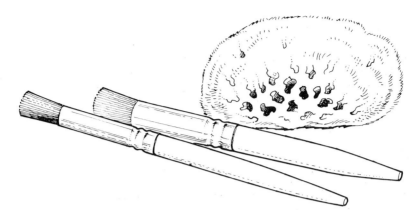

WHAT YOU WILL NEED TO GET STARTED

The art of stencilling is a simple way of adding pattern and colour to walls, floors, furniture and fabrics. Before you actually start creating designs though it is a good idea to familiarise yourself with the various stencil materials and tools you will be using. Once you know how they all work you will find that you progress much more rapidly.

Stencil Materials

The stencil itself must be hardwearing and impervious, and can be made from various materials. If you have bought the Osmiroid Stencilling Kit, open it up, and lay everything out in front of you on a table. You will see that it includes stencils made from a transparent material called acetate. Acetate is a plastic sheet which comes in a range of thicknesses. It is suitable for all kinds of stencilling projects from floors to fabrics and is extremely durable. Being transparent it is a particularly good choice for those creating their own stencils – designs can be simply traced directly on to it using permanent or India ink before cutting out. And when it comes to applying paint any build-up of colour on acetate stencils can be easily spotted and quickly cleaned off.

Stencil card is a heavy grade dark yellow coloured paper, traditionally used for stencils. It has been pre-soaked in linseed oil which gives it a smooth, impervious surface and makes it easy to cut. It can be drawn on with pencil and ink, but because it is opaque, designs must be transferred on to it using carbon paper before cutting.

It is also possible to buy stencil paper, which can be used for light, intricate stencilling. This semi-transparent material is coated with wax on both sides so will not register pencil or ink marks. When creating your own stencils it is necessary to cut directly from a pattern underneath the paper. Stencil paper is only suitable for small projects and is not very durable.

Applicators

It is always best to invest in the best brushes that you can afford; they will give consistently good results and last longer. Look for thick flexible bristles, firmly secured in a comfortable handle.

Take a look at the brushes in your stencil kit; the bristles have a round shape resembling a man's shaving brush. These can be made from hogshair or synthetic fibres, and are cut bluntly across the end to make them the correct shape for the characteristic 'pouncing' movement used when stencilling. Practice this vertical dabbing motion with the brushes from you kit, holding them like a pencil, with your fingers close to the bristles.

Stencil brushes come in various sizes from 6 - 50mm, you should choose them according to the size of the stencil opening; small openings only require small brushes.

The traditional brush gives the finished stencil a stippled look. If you wish to experiment with different applicators however it is possible to achieve other effects. Using a natural sponge for instance will create a random splashed effect; small pieces of fabric can give a soft watermarked look, and paint pads and rollers a flatter base colour.

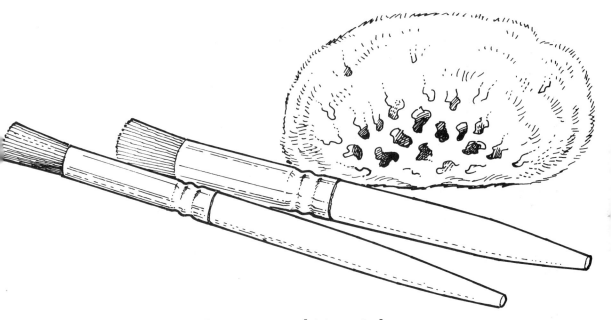

Paints and Varnishes

To be suitable for stencilling a paint must dry quickly. This means you will be able to apply additional colours or varnish without delay. It should also be creamy in texture – thin, watery paint can seep under a stencil and give a messy edge to your motif.

Acrylic Poster Paint Acrylic poster paints are generally considered the best all round stencilling medium. Widely available, they come in a good choice of colours and have a thick creamy consistency. Being water soluble they dry quickly to a matt finish. They are very versatile and can be used on all kinds of surfaces including plaster walls, woods, non-dry cleanable fabrics, unglazed ceramics, natural woven fibres like baskets, and some plastics. Acrylics are an expensive choice however for all-over wall patterns. Ordinary poster colours are a cheaper alternative.

Japan Paints Generally only available from specialist suppliers, but because of their fast drying nature and wide selection of colours they make an ideal stencil paint. Unlike acrylics they are oil based and so soluble with white spirit. They can be used on shiny non-porous surfaces such as metal, glass, glazed ceramics and laminates.

Textile Paints Available from craft shops and large department stores these are designed specifically for use on fabrics. They are fast-drying and will not wash off or disintegrate when carefully dry cleaned.

Stencil Crayons Stencil crayons are relatively new to this country and only available from specialist suppliers. Although oil-based they dry reasonably quickly and can be used for most stencilling projects.

Spray Paints Generally cellulose based, these can be used without applicators to create soft, misty looks. They dry almost instantly but require a practised hand for good results.

Domestic Emulsion Paints Standard domestic emulsion paints can also be used for stencilling. Inexpensive, easy-to-use and fast drying they can be applied to most porous surfaces including plaster, wood and unglazed ceramics. Silk or satin finish emulsions are generally tougher than matt, but a thin coat of varnish can be applied to protect surfaces against wear and tear.

Proprietary Wood Stains Can also be used to create stencil patterns on furniture and floors. They are available in an array of colours and simply tint wood allowing the grain to show through.

Varnishes Protect stencils against wear and tear. Polyurethane varnish is suitable for walls, woodwork, floors and furniture, and is available in a choice of matt, semi-gloss and gloss versions. For general use matt or semi-gloss finishes are preferable – they dry with little or no shine and do not alter the finished appearance of the stencil.

N.B. If you are working with spray paints you must only use special spray varnishes – using a brush would smudge the designs.

Extra Items

Keep a soft pencil and ruler handy for accurate marking and positioning of stencils – a plumb line is useful for checking that any patterns on walls are straight. Hold the stencil firmly in place with masking tape – this is better than ordinary tape as it peels off without damaging the surface.

When painting the stencil use a different saucer or tray for each colour, and make sure you have a bottle of the appropriate solvent and plenty of clean rags on hand.

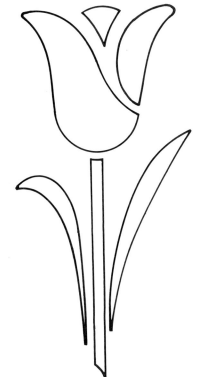

If you intend to make up your own stencils you will also need to equip yourself with a fine felt tip pen, fine gauge knitting needle and supply of tracing and carbon paper for transferring designs onto the stencil card. A craft knife with replaceable blades is best for cutting out stencil designs.

The Different Types of Stencil

Single Stencils The simplest type of stencil is one which gives you the complete pattern of the motif. Once the stencil is painted the design is finished, but you can of course repeat single stencils to create a series of the same image. This kind of stencil is usually printed in only one colour.

Symmetrical outlines such as the heart shown here can be simply cut out as a whole. More complex single stencils like the tulip need bridging areas or links between the cut out shapes to give definition to the design. These bridges also help to strengthen the stencil and prevent it becoming distorted when it is painted.

Modular Stencils This type of stencil is just one of many, used to form a complete design. So for example if you were painting a chest with a motif of acorns and oak leaves, you could use separate stencils for the leaves, stem and acorns. This would allow you to position each modular stencil where you wished, to produce a more random design, and would also mean you could work with stencils of a more manageable size.

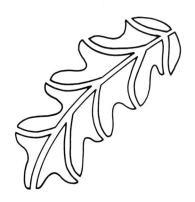

Multiple Stencils By using more complex multiple stencils you can introduce several colours into a motif. You can also eliminate the need for bridges, and divide complex vulnerable shapes into sturdier sections less likely to tear or break.

Because multiple stencils involve one stencil being printed on top of another, some method of registration is necessary to prevent overlapping and messy end results. With clear acetate one or two key lines from other parts of the design are simply drawn onto each stencil and these are then aligned when you start painting. Try laying the different acetate sheets for each design on top of one another and see how they all align.

Because oiled stencil board is opaque, a different method of registration has to be used. Each stencil has a notch cut into it in exactly the same position and when painting the design you simply make a small pencil mark through this notch on the surface to be decorated, and match up each stencil in turn.

HOW TO
STENCIL

Important Preparations

For best results make sure that the surface to be stencilled is clean and fully prepared. Wood and plaster should be carefully sanded down and any cracks or holes filled in. Fabrics must be cleaned and ironed and then stretched taut over a board to make stencilling easier. Unusual surfaces like leather, ceramic and metal will accept stencil designs provided they are clean and dry. For more detailed preparation instructions see the four special projects starting on page 45.

Work Areas

You will be able to work much quicker and more efficiently if all the equipment that you need is close to hand. Start by having everything out neatly around you. The Osmiroid kit has most of the basics, but there are one or two other items you will need to add. The stencils for all the motifs we show are included in the kit, or you can trace the designs and cut your own stencils following the instructions given later in the book.

Basic Equipment:

- Pencil and ruler for marking the position of your stencil
- Masking tape for attaching the stencil
- Paint and relevant solvent
- An old spoon and several small plates for mixing paint
- Plenty of clean rags and paper towels
- Stencil brushes
- Pad of test paper
- The stencil

Choose your work area carefully too – make sure there is plenty of natural light and that you have enough space to sit or stand comfortably. Now you can begin to stencil.

Mixing Paint

The key to successful stencilling lies in the consistency of your paint. If the paint is too dry you will hardly see the finished design, and if it is too wet the paint will seep under the stencil opening, giving it a smudged, messy look. Careful mixing of paints is therefore very important.

Stencilling uses up very little paint so it is best to start off by mixing up just a small quantity – you can always mix more later if you need to.

The only way to tell if your paint is correctly mixed is to keep testing it until you can make a perfect print like the one in our picture.

How to test your paint:

Taking a clean, dry brush, dip its bristles into the paint and then jab it vigorously onto some soft paper towels. This helps to remove excess paint and also distribute it evenly through the bristles. Repeat this action until the brush leaves a soft, shaded mark. Now use the brush to print a small area of stencil on a clean piece of scrap paper.

Try the paint undiluted to begin with, gradually blending in small amounts of the appropriate solvent if it is too dry, to bring it to the correct consistency. Don't forget to write down exactly how much solvent you add in case you need to mix up more paint.

It's important to get the consistency of the paint just right.

Too wet

Too dry

Just right

Colour Choice

Whilst on the subject of paints, it is worth briefly mentioning the effect of different colours when used together. Colours stencilled onto white or lightly tinted surfaces will retain their original tone and stand out prominantly from their backgrounds. Medium coloured backgrounds tend to absorb some of the colours of a stencil, giving them a softer, muted look. The darker a background is the more a colour will be absorbed, so if you want a motif to really stand out you must choose bright, contrasting paint colours.

Test Stencils

Once you have got the paint to the correct consistency, practise painting the stencil motif on a piece of scrap paper. This allows you to check whether any last minute alterations need to be made to the design and also gives you a chance to familiarise yourself with the basic techniques of stencilling. It is better to make your mistakes on scrap paper than the furniture or walls you have carefully prepared.

Attaching the Stencil

A stencil must be firmly secured on the surface to be stencilled. This stops it from slipping around as you work and helps prevent paint seeping under the edges of the template and smudging the motif.

Taking the stencil in your hand, carefully position it on the test paper or surface to be stencilled. Check that it is completely flat and then attach it with small pieces of masking tape.

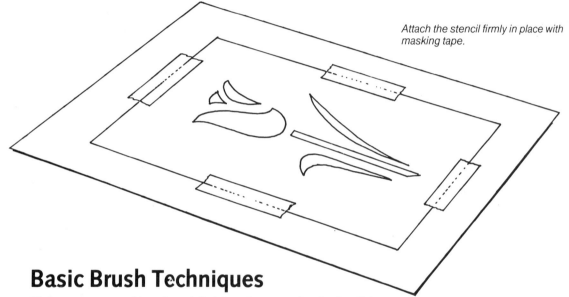

Attach the stencil firmly in place with masking tape.

Basic Brush Techniques

Pick up your stencil brush and dip it into the pre-mixed paint. Take off any surplus by working the brush up and down on paper towels. It will be ready for stencilling when the mark it leaves is soft and evenly shaded. Patchy blobs of colour mean that there is still too much paint on the brush and you must continue jabbing away until you have distributed the paint evenly through its bristles.

Holding the brush like a pencil, with your fingers close to the bristles you can now begin to apply colour through the cut areas of the stencil. Keep your wrist flexible and relaxed as you dab the brush up and down 'pouncing' or stippling the colour onto the surface. Use your other hand to hold the stencil flat and stop the bristles of the brush catching on any intricately cut areas.

Aim to build up your colour gradually, rather than putting it on too thickly and then trying to rub it off. Start at the edges of the stencil, forming the general outline and then work your way into the centre using broad circular movements, clockwise and anti-clockwise until the shapes are filled in.

A pretty four colour stencil effectively
frames this doorway to the kitchen.

SMALLBONE KITCHENS

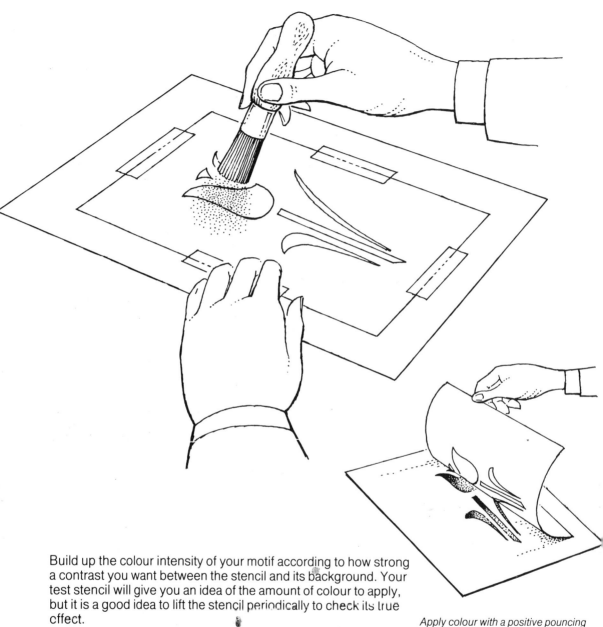

Build up the colour intensity of your motif according to how strong a contrast you want between the stencil and its background. Your test stencil will give you an idea of the amount of colour to apply, but it is a good idea to lift the stencil periodically to check its true effect.

When you are satisfied with the results remove the stencil, lifting it vertically to ensure you do not smudge any areas of the design still wet. Leave the paint to dry before adding any further colours. Remember to wipe excess paint from the stencil each time you finish a motif, and when you have completed a project make sure all your equipment is thoroughly cleaned and put away.

Apply colour with a positive pouncing action carefully lifting the stencil periodically to check its true effect.

Protecting the Surface

If the surface you have stencilled is likely to be subjected to a certain amount of wear and tear it is a good idea to give it a protective coat of varnish. This not only helps prolong the life of the design but also preserves its good looks.

Positioning Stencils

With some stencilling projects, decorating a small box or making a bookmark for example, you may be able to place motifs using the judgement of your eyes. Designs placed casually like this can also be used to great effect in some informal interiors – simple motifs and borders adding their own naive charm to a room.

Most large, repeat stencil designs however must be accurately measured and marked out.

Centering a design:

1. Find the centre of the surface to be stencilled by drawing diagonal lines from opposite corners. Mark with a pencil cross.

2. Repeat the same procedure on the stencil itself.

3. Align the two cross marks and print.

Marking out a border:

Measure the position of your border accurately at several points along the walls length, marking each point in soft pencil.

1. Decide roughly where you want your border to be then using a ruler and soft pencil measure accurately in from the edge at several points along its length. Mark each point.

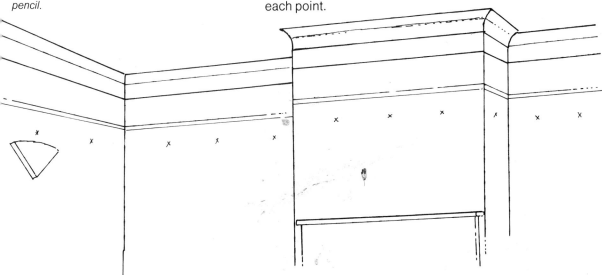

2. Join the points together to give a continuous registration line along the surface and make a corresponding mark on your stencil so that you can align the two accurately when painting.

3. To ensure that the finished border looks equally balanced find the centre of the surface to be decorated, as already described.

4. Measure the width of the stencil template then starting at the centre of the surface, work out exactly how many times it can be repeated across it. Don't forget to include the spacing between motifs in your calculation.

5. If you finish on partial patterns at either end, try altering the spaces between the motifs until you are able to fit in the complete pattern. If this proves too difficult you may be able to adapt the design slightly at the edges to fit the space available.

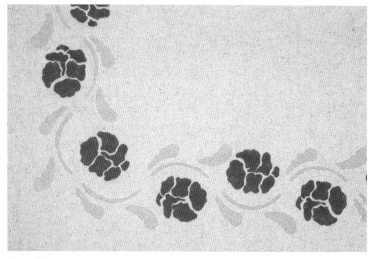

One method of dealing with a corner by gently curving the design.

Handling corners: When a border design leads into a corner there are several different ways of carrying the design on:-

1. Turn the template at a right angle so that you butt one motif against another.

2. Mitre the motif itself. To do this draw a diagonal line at the corner, place masking tape on one side and stencil the border right up to the tape. Reposition the stencil on the other side of the line and complete the pattern. Remove the tape.

3. Continue the design around the corner by blocking in and filling out certain shapes to produce a gently curved design.

A delicate scallop motif brings this washbasin to life.

4. Design a special corner piece using shapes from the border itself. Stencil these corner pieces first, then measure and space the borders to fit afterwards.

All over patterns: Where a stencil pattern is to be repeated many times in an all over pattern (on a length of fabric for example) you will need to mark out an accurate grid on the surface to be stencilled.

1. Start off by checking that the motif is accurately positioned in the centre of your stencil template.

2. With the help of some graph paper mark on the template the same sized square or rectangle that is to be used in your grid.

3. Square off the surface to be stencilled by finding the centre then working outwards to each side, marking squares or rectangles corresponding in size to those on your stencil template. For accuracy it is best to use a ruler and T square or a plumb line.

4. Using the marks on your template as a guide, position your designs within the grid and stencil.

Mark out all over patterns first using a squared grid.

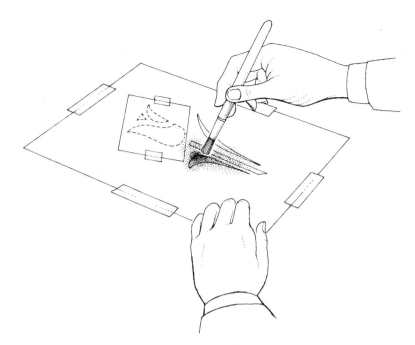

CREATING SPECIAL STENCIL EFFECTS

Once you have learnt the basics of stencilling you may want to experiment with some slightly different techniques to give your designs a special look.

Applying Two or More Colours

Single Stencils

Most multi-colour designs use a series of registered overlays, but in some cases it is possible to apply more than one colour through a single stencil template.

Simple shapes with broad bridges or links give the best results. Using a small stencil brush carefully apply each colour through the cut areas of the template – the bridges themselves will act as your guard keeping the different colours separate. Stencils with narrow bridges need a specially made guard to keep colours separate. This guard can be made from a strip of stencil card or a piece of masking tape which has had some of its stickiness removed by pressing it repeatedly onto a piece of clean fabric. Use your guard to cover the areas of adjacent stencil that you do not want to paint.

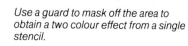

Use a guard to mask off the area to obtain a two colour effect from a single stencil.

Multiple Stencils

On page 12 we explained what multiple stencils are and the principles of how they work. To use these stencils start by laying each of the component templates out in front of you. The Osmiroid stencilling kit includes multiple stencils made from acetate. Take one out to experiment with. You will see that each component stencil template fits exactly on top of the next, with every part of the design perfectly in alignment. Start by taking one of these templates and securing it in place. (Stencils made from opaque card will have registration notches on either side – make a pencil mark against these). Print the stencil as normal, leave to dry and remove. Tape the second stencil in place carefully aligning the design underneath or matching up the pencil registration marks and print. Continue in this way until the stencil design is complete.

Remember: Always finish painting everything in one colour and let it fully dry before moving on to the next shade.

- Use a fresh brush for each colour.
- Erase any pencil marks from your finished design.

Shaded Stencils

One of the basic rules of stencilling is to build colour up gradually as you paint. With a little practise you can soon learn how to vary the intensity of colour on a simple stencil shape, to give it a three dimensional quality.

Practise shading the intensity of colour on a simple stencil to obtain a three dimensional effect.

When you become more confident about stencilling try using additional colours through the same stencil opening to create a highlighted or shaded effect.

The first step is to apply an even coat of paint. Once this is dry to the touch apply a lighter or darker tone of the initial colour, working your way from one edge of the stencil to the other. You should not refill your brush with paint. As it becomes lighter it blends in with the first colour to give you a more natural shaded quality.

For the most realistic results study the way light falls on objects around you. As a general rule dark colours applied near the base give a shaded effect, light ones near the top add highlights.

Different Brush Strokes

The traditional pouncing action used when applying paint for stencilling produces a finished design with a characteristic stippled or orange peel effect. If you want to give your work a softer look try using one of these alternative brush strokes.

- Working with a very dry brush apply paint through the stencil opening using a smooth circular action.

- Starting at the edge of your stencil slide the tip of your brush into the centre of the opening. Lift the brush,

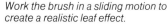

Work the brush in a sliding motion to create a realistic leaf effect.

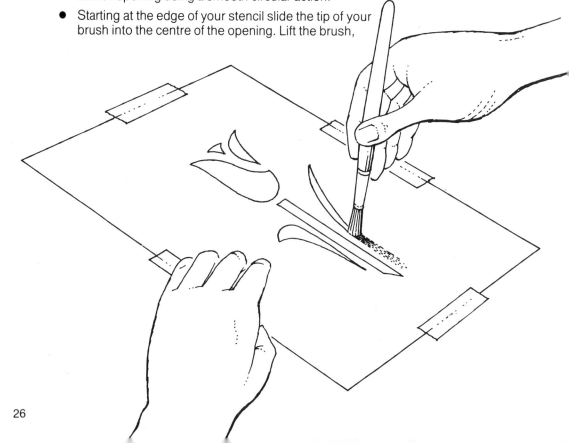

apply more paint if necessary and repeat the sliding motion from another side of the design. This technique gives a slightly veined, feathery look to stencils and is an ideal choice for leaves.

Unusual Applicators

You can also give your work a different look by using other applicators to colour the stencil.

Natural sponges make good alternatives to stencil brushes.

Natural sponges available from most chemists make good alternatives to stencil brushes. They give finished motifs a textural, mottled appearance which can vary according to the grade of sponge used. Fine, cosmetic sponges create a gentle, spattered look, whilst those of a coarser grade produce more open effects. More delicate textures can be achieved by building the colour up in an area with several applications of paint. Experiment with small pieces of different grade sponge using your stencils, paint and test paper.

Handy Tips:

- Work with small pieces of sponge – they are easier to manage, and less expensive to buy than larger ones.
- The sponge should be moist but not wet when being used – remove excess paint on to paper towels before beginning.
- Use the same dabbing motion as you would when working with a brush, but apply less pressure. This will produce a delicate spattered look and allow you to vary the intensity of colour as you wish.

Fabric can also be used to apply paint through a stencil opening. Velvet and velour create a soft, watercolour effect, but it is worth experimenting with a variety of fabrics to learn what finished effects they produce. Use the stencils and paint in your kits.

Handy Tips:

- Work with small pieces of fabric.
- Using your index finger like a brush, wrap the fabric round it and dip it into the paint. Remove excess colour on clean paper towels.
- Rub the material across the stencil opening from the edges to the centre, applying a gentle pressure.

In addition to sponges and fabric it is also possible to apply colour to stencils using eye shadow applicators, decorators paint pads and rollers. Use your paints and stencils to experiment. Remember there are no set rules to follow.

A stencilled frieze on a softly sponged background echoes the design of the tiles behind.

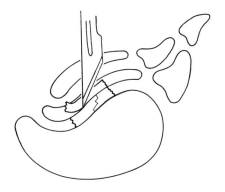

CORRECTING MISTAKES

If you make a mistake when you are stencilling don't panic – most can be quickly and easily corrected.

Paint Smudges and Drips

- Keep a special 'kneadable' rubber (available from art suppliers) to hand, and use it to swab up small smudges and drips. It is generally best to wait until the paint is almost dry or you may smudge it even more.
- Clean cotton buds are good for picking up drips of paint. Any stain left can be treated as above.
- Save a small pot of the background paint – it can be used for disguising stubborn marks if necessary.
- If your background has a wood stained finish apply a protective coat of clear varnish over it before stencilling so that errors can be easily wiped off.

Paint Runs

- Start by removing the stencil and wiping all the paint off it with a damp rag.
- If the paint run has simply made the edges of your design fuzzy, try neatening it up with your kneaded rubber. If this doesn't work shift the stencil over very slightly and re-stencil to sharpen the edges.
- If the paint run is extensive you will have to wipe off that area altogether using a cloth moistened with the appropriate solvent. Protect other areas of the print with masking tape or strips of stencil card.
- If the whole print is ruined you will need to wipe it all off with solvent, repaint the background and start again.

Faults in the Design

- Small mistakes in an all-over pattern or border will not generally be apparent, and are best left un-touched.
- Minor misjudgements in the placement of designs can be dealt with in any of the ways already mentioned.
- Disastrous mistakes are best wiped off and painted over before re-stencilling.
- Gaps in the printed stencil may be caused by stencil shapes that are cut too small. Mark the problem area on the stencil template and trim it to the proper size.
- Designs that simply look unfinished can often be rectified by improvisation. Using parts of your stencil,

fill in any gaps or unbalanced areas with small elements of the designs.

Note: If you practise first with a test stencil as we suggest, any design faults can be rectified before it gets to this stage.

The Importance of Cleaning

- It is easy for your hands to get covered with paint whilst you are working. Try to keep them as clean as possible to prevent accidental smudging.

- Don't allow your brushes to become clogged with paint; they will lose their flexibility.

- Keep the stencil template as clean as possible – an excessive build up of paint will gradually reduce the size of your design and eventually obliterate intricate detailing.

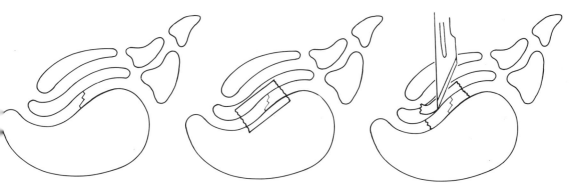

Three simple steps to repairing a damaged stencil.

Repairing a Stencil

Torn stencils can be easily repaired.

- If the bridging link has been torn, but is still attached to the stencil, hold it carefully in place and secure it with pieces of masking or clear, strong adhesive tape on both sides. Trim away any excess tape as shown.

- If a section of stencil has been torn right off you must replace it. First trace around the shape of the broken piece onto a small piece of stencil material. Cut out the replacement and tape it in place as above. Trim off any excess tape.

Floor stencilling adds interest to a plain wooden floor and is a cheaper alternative to carpets.

MAKING YOUR OWN STENCILS

With the stencils in the Osmiroid kit you will quickly be able to master the basic techniques of stencilling and gain confidence in your skills. Once you have practised with these however and decorated several surfaces you will want to create some new designs of your own. You may wish for instance to decorate a room to match the pattern of the fabric used for the curtains. Your stencil design could be adapted to form a wall border, all-over floor pattern or simple motif on a piece of furniture.

On your first few attempts it is best to stick to simple designs. Single, symmetrical shapes – leaves, squares, triangles and so on are the easiest stencils to make. Once you feel a bit more proficient you can move on to more complex un-symmetrical motifs. Inspiration for your designs can come from many sources – magazine photographs, fabrics, gift wrap, flowers and even animals.

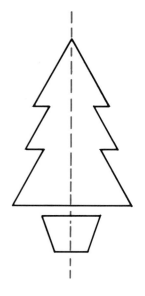

Easy Steps to Creating Your Own Stencils

1. Make up a master pattern by laying a sheet of tracing paper over your design and tracing it with a soft lead pencil.

2. Create the bridges that will hold the stencil together and give definition to the design. Place another sheet of tracing paper over the master pattern, then using the illustrations below as a guide start to create bridges, dividing individual components of the design into a

Make use of bridges to give definition to your designs.

*Take your inspiration for stencil designs
from simple shapes like flower petals.*

series of shapes that can be easily cut out as a flat pattern. Use the contours and natural shading of objects as a guide to the lines you draw, broadening them to form the bridges. Make these bridges as narrow as possible but never less than 3mm. Try to simplify complex designs – the finished stencil will be easier to work with and less visually confusing. Part of the charm of stencilling is that it produces the impression of real life objects rather than an exact replica.

3. Make a permanent image by going over all the lines of your final design with a black felt-tipped marker.

4. Work out how much stencil material you need to use. Cut it to fit the size of your stencil design, allowing a margin of at least 3 to 5cm around the edge to give strength and rigidity.

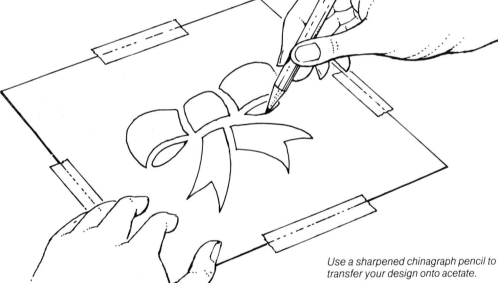

Use a sharpened chinagraph pencil to transfer your design onto acetate.

5. Transfer the design onto your chosen stencil material. If you are working with acetate, simply lay the sheet directly over your design and secure it in place with small pieces of masking tape. Use a sharpened chinagraph pencil, fine felt-tipped or technical drawing pen to transfer the image onto the acetate.

With stencil board or waxed paper the easiest way to transfer the design is to sandwich carbon paper (carbon side down) between it and the board, securing it firmly with masking tape. Using a very hard pencil or the tip of a fine gauge knitting needle trace around the outline. Remove the carbon paper and then go over the image left on the stencil board with a fine, dark fibre tipped pen or sharp pencil. Tracing paper can be used as an alternative to carbon paper – you must first trace the design, go over it on the reverse side with a soft graphite pencil, and then transfer this layer of graphite onto the board.

6. Cut the stencil out. Start by fixing the acetate, oiled card or paper to your cutting board. (If you are working with acetate it is helpful to lay a piece of white paper underneath the sheet so you can see what you are doing). Secure it firmly in place with pieces of masking tape to stop it slipping around when you work.

Using your craft knife like a pencil, begin cutting the design keeping a smooth continuous movement.

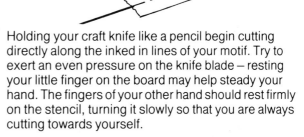

Holding your craft knife like a pencil begin cutting directly along the inked in lines of your motif. Try to exert an even pressure on the knife blade – resting your little finger on the board may help steady your hand. The fingers of your other hand should rest firmly on the stencil, turning it slowly so that you are always cutting towards yourself.

Take you time – practise lifting your cutting blade as little as possible, the object is to keep up a smooth continuous movement.

Tips

- Start cutting in the middle of your design, it will retain its strength better.
- Deal with small shapes before moving on to large ones.
- Always work with a sharp blade – blunt knives will slip and be hard to control. They are dangerous too.
- When you are cutting a curved or circular shape, move the card or acetate around the blade, not the blade around the card – this allows you to keep up the fluid cutting action.
- Don't panic if you cut past an outline by mistake. Stop and seal it on both sides with masking or clear adhesive tape, making sure you trim away any excess.
- Once the cutting is complete turn the stencil over and smooth any rough or uneven edges with fine sandpaper.

Multiple Stencils

Cutting multiple stencils is a simple progression from basic single colour templates.

Starting at the design stage you must decide on the colours of individual elements of the motif. It is a good idea to make yourself a rough sketch to check that the colour combinations work together. Try not to complicate your design with too many colours, remember each colour requires a different stencil template.

A simple fruit stencil has been adapted to give three pattern variations that decorate this hallway.

Start by cutting three pieces of stencil card, paper or acetate to size, remembering to allow a 5cm border around the edge. With clear acetate and waxed paper the procedure for transferring the components of the design is easy. Simply tape first one sheet, then the others over the design in the order shown, tracing around each colour in turn. Remember to draw in a few basic lines from the motif each time for accurate alignment when it comes to painting. Mark each sheet with its colour.

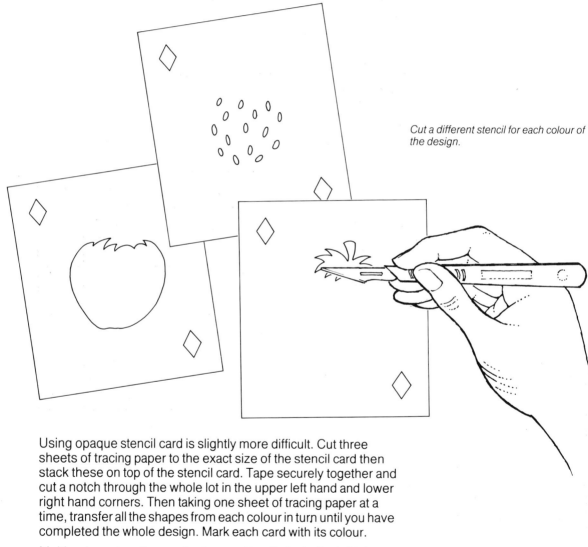

Cut a different stencil for each colour of the design.

Using opaque stencil card is slightly more difficult. Cut three sheets of tracing paper to the exact size of the stencil card then stack these on top of the stencil card. Tape securely together and cut a notch through the whole lot in the upper left hand and lower right hand corners. Then taking one sheet of tracing paper at a time, transfer all the shapes from each colour in turn until you have completed the whole design. Mark each card with its colour.

Multi-colour stencils can also be used to eliminate the bridging links in a design, and to divide intricate shapes into sturdier sections less likely to tear.

Changing the Size of Your Designs

You may wish to change the size of a design, enlarging a small section of a border pattern for instance to make a motif for a piece of furniture. The easiest way to reduce or enlarge designs is by using a photocopying machine. Most local libraries have one for public use.

If you don't have access to a photocopier you can change the size of designs using the grid method. With a pencil and ruler draw an accurately scaled grid over your original drawing, using for instance a scale of 6cm. To reduce the size of the design simply draw up another grid with squares of 3cm and carefully copy the motif one square at a time. To enlarge a picture simply do the same thing with a grid of 12cm squares and so on.

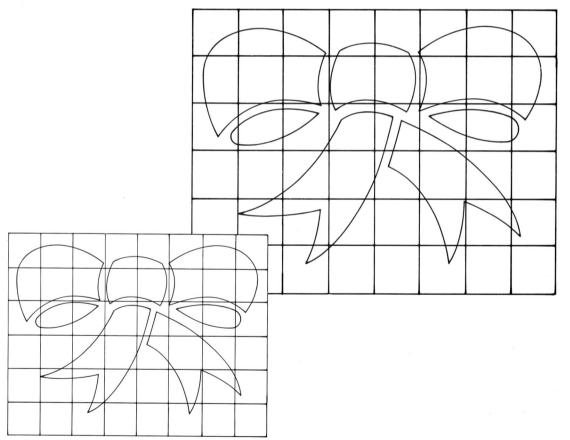

You can reduce or enlarge your motif by drawing an accurately spaced grid over your original design.

Choosing the Stencil Material

We have already looked briefly at the differences between the three main stencil materials in the section of What You Will Need to Get Started. The following serves to remind you of the characteristics before you make your choice.

Acetate

- Clear plastic sheet available in several thicknesses.
- Designs can be traced directly onto acetate, so there is no need for tracing or carbon paper.
- Although quite expensive it is durable and will last for many years.
- It has a certain flexibility, but will crack if roughly handled.
- Paint build-up can be easily cleaned.
- Ideal for multi-colour stencils which require several overlays.
- Beginners should work only with simple shapes – acetate can be more difficult to cut than oiled card or waxed paper.

Stencil Card

- Opaque yellow card which has been soaked in linseed oil, making it waterproof.
- Designs cannot be traced directly onto the card, they must be transferred using carbon or tracing paper.
- It is inexpensive yet reasonably durable.
- Stencil card has good flexibility.
- After successive uses stencil card does tend to become clogged with paint.
- Ideal for beginners it is easy to cut.
- Good for small and intricate designs.

Stencil Paper

- Semi-transparent thick paper which has a layer of wax on either side.
- Designs can generally be cut by placing them directly under the stencil paper.

The vibrant choice of paints in these stencil designs reflect the colours of the rustic china displayed on the dresser.

CROWN PAINTS

43

- Inexpensive but has limited lifespan.
- Stencil paper is flexible but will tear if treated roughly.
- Paint build-up is difficult to remove.
- Ideal for small one-off stencils.
- Good choice for beginners to practise designs.
- Not recommended for multi-colour stencils.

STENCIL
PROJECTS

The following projects are designed to help you master the basic techniques of stencilling, to build your confidence and to inspire you to design and cut your own patterns. Each project has simple step-by-step instructions and offers information on the preparation for backgrounds and suggestions for protective finishing if necessary.

The stencils for all the motifs we show are included in the Osmiroid Stencilling Kit, or you can trace the designs and cut your own stencils following the instructions given earlier in the book, reducing or enlarging them as you wish to suit different applications.

Take your time and enjoy yourself, you'll be delighted to learn how easy stencilling is.

Project 1 Stencilling onto Paper

Use the floral stencil design to decorate hand-made greeting cards, stationery for special occasions, or to ornament a bookplate for the front of a favourite book. The instructions we give here are for a bookmark, but can easily be adapted for other applications.

Materials

Card cut into bookmark shape
Pre-cut single poppy stencil from kit
Paint and water
Plate for mixing paint
Brush
Masking tape
Paper towels
Test paper

Surface Preparation

None required.

Method

1. Start by laying all your equipment neatly out in front of you.

2. If you don't have the Osmiroid kit, transfer and cut out the stencil design as explained on page 36.

3. Mix your chosen paint colour to the correct consistency following the instructions given on page 14. Test the paint colour on a piece of scrap paper until the brush leaves a soft, shaded look.

4. Practise using the paint with your stencil on a test sheet of paper, holding your brush like a pencil, and using the characteristic pouncing action described on page 16. Examine the test print for any paint runs, smudges or drips. If there are any problems adjust the consistency of your paint and make sure your brush has less on it next time. When you are happy with the quality of the finished result you can move on to the real stencil.

5. Place your cleaned stencil in the centre of the bookmark and hold in position with masking tape. Using the techniques you have learnt in the book, print your stencil. Remember to work your way in from the edges of the stencil, using broad circular movements.

6. Allow the paint to dry then peel off the masking tape and remove the stencil. Leave the bookmark to dry thoroughly overnight.

7. You have completed your first stencil project. Your finished bookmark requires no special sealing.

Remember: Always work with a dry brush, you can go over the stencil several times to build up colour, but it is not so easy to remove an excess of paint once applied.

Project 2 Stencilling onto Fabric

Using stencilled patterns on fabrics gives you the chance to create your very own textiles. Start with simple projects – a single motif applied to plain cushions or a border edging a set of table mats. When you get more proficient you will be able to adapt patterns from the walls and floors that you have stencilled in a room, to make fabric for curtains and blinds. Suitable fabrics include cotton, linen, cotton/polyester and silk. Heavily textured and knitted fabrics are best avoided.

Using the two-colour poppy border motif, we give you instructions here for printing the stencil onto a curtain.

Materials

Curtain material
Pre-cut poppy border stencil from kit
2 × paint colours and water
2 × plates for mixing paint
2 × brushes
Masking tape
Paper towels
Test paper
Chalk for marking stencil position

Surface Preparation

1. Pre-wash the curtain material according to the printed instructions. This will remove any special finishes applied during manufacture.
2. Press the curtain material carefully.

Method

1. Spread all your stencilling equipment out in front of you.
2. Transfer and cut the two component stencils if necessary, following our guide on page 36. Mark each clearly A or B to match our illustrations.
3. Lay the curtain material on to a clean, flat work surface, and tape it firmly in place, gently stretching it so that it is completely smooth.
4. Decide where you want to place your design on the curtain. Mark out the position for your border using the instructions on page 19.
5. Mix your two paint colours to the correct consistency according to our guide on page 14.
6. Starting with template A, lay it in position on the curtain, aligning it carefully with any chalk position marks, and tape in place.
7. Dip your first brush into the paint colour for stencil A, remove the excess onto paper towels and pounce colour through the stencil openings. Work the paint slowly into the fibres of the fabric to obtain an even print.
8. Remove the stencil gently, then re-align for the next position – print. Continue in this way until you have completed all the motifs in the first colour.
9. Taking stencil B, lay it in position on top of your initial print, align the registration marks precisely and tape in place. Print as before, using the second clean brush.
10. Continue as with previous colour until you have finished the border.
11. Allow the paint to completely dry – 7 days if you are using the acrylic poster paint. Heat set the paint using a cool iron. Place a clean tea towel over the stencil and hold the iron on it for about 30 seconds.

Remember: Make sure you print all the stencils in colour A before moving to the colours for stencil B.

Project 3 Stencilling onto Furniture

Small pieces of furniture are a good choice for first projects. They can be prepared and painted with minimum amount of mess. Stencilled motifs and borders can be used to great effect on old chests of drawers, tables and chairs, but never use them on genuine antiques, you will ruin their value.

Our third stencil project uses the single colour shell border to decorate a bathroom cupboard.

Materials

Cupboard
Coarse and fine sandpaper
Wood glue and filler
Paintbrush
Base paint or wood stain
Pre-cut shell stencil from kit
Paint and water
Plate for mixing paint
Brush
Masking tape
Clear polyurethane varnish
Paper towels
Test paper
Pencil and ruler for marking stencil position

Surface Preparation

1. For best results spend time sanding down the surface of the old paint or wood with first coarse and then fine sandpaper. Particularly old or damaged paint and varnish may need to be stripped off completely using a proprietary stripper following manufacturers' instructions.

2. Check that old pieces of furniture are free from woodworm, glue together any loose joints and fill any cracks or holes with wood filler. Finish with a light sanding.

3. Paint the furniture with a base coat of paint or proprietary wood stain.

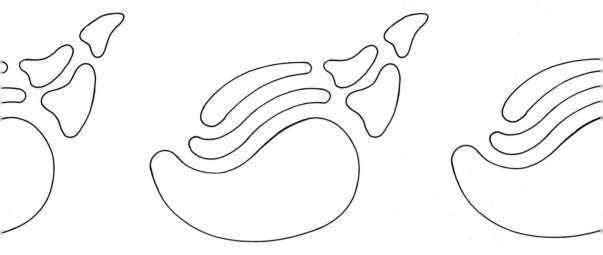

Method

1. Lay out all the tools and equipment needed in your work area. Spread plenty of paper down to protect the floor and place the furniture to be stencilled on top of it.

2. Prepare your own stencils, if necessary following the instructions on page 34. Remember to mark each component template with registration marks and the appropriate paint colours.

3. Find out how many times your border design will be repeated along the cupboard, using the instructions for positioning patterns on page 19. Remember to find the middle of each edge on the cupboard, working out the position of your design by starting from this point and making your way to each corner. Measure and mark out the line of your stencil pattern along the front of the cupboard.

4. Mix up the paint colour to the correct consistency as before and test on a sheet of paper.

Remember single motifs don't need to be placed in the centre of a surface, they may look better in one corner only or repeated on opposite sides.

5. Pick up the design, tape it in position over the first set of placement marks and apply paint colour. Remove and realign for the next position – print. Carry on in this way until you have completed the border.

6. When the paint has completely dried (allow 7 days for acrylic poster paint) apply a protective coat of clear polyurethane varnish.

If you feel more ambitious when you've finished this project you could carry the design on to the legs of the cupboard too.

Project 4 Stencilling onto Walls

Using stencils on walls gives you the flexibility to create all kinds of
special effects, whether it be a simple frieze at dado and picture rail
height, a border used to frame doors and windows, or a complex
all-over pattern.

Our last stencil project introduces you to a two colour clown
design, ideal for a small child's bedroom. We suggest you start by
using it as a frieze at dado height, but there are many other
possible positions for wall stencils.

Materials

Sandpaper
All-purpose filler
Paintbrush
Paint for base coat
Pre-cut clown stencil from kit
2 × paint colours and water
2 × plates for mixing paint
2 × brushes
Masking tape
Paper towels
Test paper
Chalk, ruler and plumb line for marking stencil position

Surface Preparation

1. Make sure that the walls to be stencilled are clean,
   smooth and dry.

2. If the existing paintwork or wall covering is sound then
   simply brush clean and apply a fresh base coat of paint.

3. Small areas of peeling paint and damaged wallpaper
   can usually be smoothed over, but if the surface is in
   very poor condition it may be better to strip it back to
   bare plaster. Fill any cracks and holes with filler and
   sand over once this has dried. Badly cracked plaster
   should be covered with lining paper prior to painting.

4. New plasterwork must have completely dried out.
   Remove any spatters left by the plasterer with a
   scraper, but do not sand. Apply a coat of sealant prior
   to painting to prevent any salts from the plaster
   leaching through.

Method

1. Lay out all the stencil equipment around you. Protect floors with plenty of newspaper.

2. Transfer and cut your own component stencil templates if necessary, marking the registration points and labelling each A and B as shown.

3. To position your dado border mark horizontal lines using the ceiling and skirting board as a guide. Find the centre of the wall and then work out how many border repeats will fit along its length, starting from the centre each time and working your way out to each edge as explained on page 19. Decide how you want to tackle the corners using one of the methods detailed on page 20.

*Stencils used to decorate a complete
room.*

Starting with stencil A from your kit tape it in position and print. Reposition the stencil and print in its next position, continuing in this way until you have completed everything in the first colour.

5. Move on to stencil B, positioning and printing all motifs in the second colour, carefully re-aligning them on top of the first motif each time.

6. Allow the completed border to dry thoroughly (around 7 days with acrylic poster paint). Paints can then be left untreated or given a thin coat of clear matt varnish for protection.

Remember

- Always use a clean brush for each paint colour.
- Finish everything in one colour before moving on to the next.

CLOSING WORDS

Now you have tried the four stencil projects we have set, we hope you will feel confident and enthusiastic to try your hand at some more ambitious projects. Happy stencilling!

Osmiroid Creative Leisure Series

Each title in the Osmiroid Creative Leisure series has been written in a lively "to the point" style, with very practical advice to ensure that exciting creative results are quickly achievable.

Chinese Brush Painting includes Chinese Calligraphy and a host of ideas from animal and plant subjects to landscapes.

Colour Calligraphy explains colour theory and shows some of the many ways that imaginative colour calligraphy can be created.

Pen and Ink Drawing leads the reader through many subjects and styles and includes enough "tricks of the trade" to ensure that everyone can create something.

The Art of Sketching shows the reader how to approach sketching from a very practical viewpoint, covering a wide range of indoor and outdoor subjects.

The Art of Poster Making shows the reader how to create posters using the wide variety of media and ideas.

Design and artwork by Nigel Long, Winchester

Printed in Spain